WILDLIFE

of

YELLOWSTONE & GRAND TETON
NATIONAL PARKS

SHING

ROCKY MOUNTAIN
WILDLIFE
of
YELLOWSTONE & GRAND TETON
NATIONAL PARKS

ISBN 0-943972-41-8
Library of Congress Catalog Card Number 95-79493
Copyright © 1995 Homestead Publishing
Printed in Hong Kong through Palace Press.

Published by
HOMESTEAD PUBLISHING
Box 193 • Moose, Wyoming 83012

PHOTOGRAPHIC CREDITS
Cover photo: Trumpeter Swan, Carl Schreier.
Title page: Moose along the Oxbow of the Snake River, Grand Teton, Rick Konrad.
Preface Page (Previous page): Misty elk in Yellowstone, Scott McKinley.
DJ Cox: 34, 38, 53, 55; Derrick Ditchburn: 48, 52 (Steller's Jay); John Fandek: 30; Raymond Gehman: 45;
Dan & Cindy Hartman: 32 (pine marten), 39, 40 (pika), 47; Henry Holdsworth: 10, 29, 42 (chipmunk),
51, 52 (tanager), 62-63; Rick Konrad: title page; Carl Oksanen/Alpen Glow Images: 20; Thomas
Mangelsen: 24; Scott McKinley: 2-3, 5, 14, 15, 18, 21, 22, 26-27, 28, 32 (weasel), 33, 36-37, 40 (snowshoe
hare), 41, 43, 44, 49, 54; Carl Schreier: front cover, 6, 7, 12-13, 16, 17, 23, 42 (red squirrel and golden
manteled ground squirrel), 46, 50 (trumpeter swan and nest), 52 (bluebird), 56, 57, 59, 60, 61, 64.

ILLUSTRATION CREDITS
Don Feaser: 58; Robert Hynes: 8-9.

DISCOVERY OF A WONDERLAND

Nearly a century and a half ago, explorers and fur traders returned from the remote regions of the Northern Rocky Mountains and astounded the American people with tales of a land of lakes, forests, mountains, and canyons where giant geysers spouted, springs boiled, and wildlife abounded. Coming from such men as Jim Bridger—a notorious teller of tall tales—these accounts were received with some skepticism. But in 1870 an expedition of distinguished citizens led by Gen. Henry Washburn returned from the "Land of the Rock Yellow River," as it was called by the Indians, confirming its marvelous character. A movement to set aside this

Even though the white-tailed jackrabbit is a rare critter and found only in the northern Ecosystem, it still is an integral part of a natural community.

wonderland for all the people was soon launched by a group of foresighted citizens. Their efforts resulted in establishment of the world's first national park.

Wildlife was recognized, in the 1872 Organic Act in which Congress set aside Yellowstone, as one of the major resources of the new park. But apparently the idea that wildlife had rights of its own, or that its survival might even be important, was slow in taking hold. For the killing of bison and other Yellowstone animals continued even after the park was established. A later act, the Lacy Act (May 7, 1894), provided, in part, "that all hunting, or the killing. . . of

/5

any bird or wild animal, except dangerous animals. . . is prohibited. . . ." It was a start, but it still allowed government bounty hunters to slaughter predators, even against Presidential decree.

The large predators were the last to gain the sanctuary that had been accorded legislatively to all animals of the park. In an effort to build up the populations of elk and bison, a prolonged campaign against mountain lions, wolves, and coyotes was instituted. The killing did not end until the early 1930s, when most species were eliminated or severely reduced.

Today, a new ecological awareness, a wider appreciation of the esthetic and scientific value of wild animals, and extensive research have led to better understanding of wildlife

Hayden Valley (above) in Yellowstone National Park, Grand Teton National Park (left) and the surrounding ecosystem are among America's prime wildlife-observation areas. This region provides the essential requirements—habitat and space—to sustain healthy wildlife populations.

populations. But, despite the mistakes of the past and the gaps in our understanding of the ecology of the parks, they are havens for wildlife and meccas for people who wish to see animals in a natural state. Indeed, Yellowstone and Grand Teton provide habitat for most of the species known to have been present when the park was established.

Your appreciation and enjoyment of Yellowstone's wild creatures will be enhanced by a better understanding of how each fits into the intricate web of plant and animal life. This book has been prepared to contribute toward this understanding and to serve as a guide to finding, observing, and photographing some of the more noticeable, more interesting, and rarer species.

WEB OF LIFE IN YELLOWSTONE AND GRAND TETON

Basic to the understanding of the web of life is the fact that plants directly or indirectly support all animal life. Chemical compounds in the soil, water, and air combined with energy from sunlight are transformed into plant growth. Plants serve as food for herbivorous animals, which in turn serve as food for carnivores. The deaths of plants and animals release chemical compounds back into the soil, water, and air for reuse in the next cycle of life.

Within this web all animals live—like people—in communities. A community is an association of plants and animals occupying a specific physical environment. Each kind of animal lives in its particular community because that environment provides its basic needs—which are the same for all animals: food, water, air (oxygen), shelter, protection from enemies, and living space. Each species fills a particular niche in the community—which might be compared to the job a person holds in a human community.

Thus, in the sagebrush-grassland community of Yellowstone, the white-tailed jackrabbit feeds on green plants and is itself food for

such predators as the coyote, red-tailed hawk, and golden eagle. In other words, its functional niche in the community is as a direct or primary consumer of green plants and as a source of food for secondary consumers. A little thought leads to the conclusion that flesh eaters, the carnivores are just as dependent on the green plants as are plant eaters, or herbivores.

Within a natural community there is some overlap among the niches occupied by the many kinds of living things. But there is usually very little direct competition between species. Thus, the jackrabbit uses some of the same food plants as the pronghorn, but the jackrabbit utilizes the lower aspects of the shrub and the pronghorn the upper portions, which are out of reach for the jackrabbit. Other adaptations allow animals to survive the changing seasons. Within Yellowstone and Grand Teton animals have a choice of either migrating, hibernating, adapting with a new coat or perishing.

The northern Rocky Mountains hosts a variety of wildlife species, including (left to right): osprey, coyote, mule deer, bighorn sheep, elk, grizzly bear, moose, ground squirrels, black bear, white pelican, scaups, bison, yellow-bellied marmot, trumpeter swan, green-winged teal and pronghorn.

Many kinds of animals make use of more than one community. Yellowstone's elk, for example, in summer can be found in nearly every plant community in the park from sagebrush-grasslands to subalpine meadows. Their natural migration prevented them from over utilizing one particular community.

Communities in a complex natural area such as Yellowstone always include many kinds of plants, a number of plant eaters, and at least a few flesh eaters. The combination of these organisms provides a system of checks and balances. Indeed, shifts in the relative numbers and distribution of the members of the community are occurring constantly as the natural environment changes. Rarely do these shifts in complex communities have drastic consequences.

DISCOVERING WILDLIFE WITH CAMERA AND BINOCULARS

Once you're on the road looking for wild animals in Yellowstone and Grand Teton, there's a simple formula that almost insures success: SLOW DOWN...STOP...LOOK... LISTEN. The rewards will be greater, however, if you familiarize yourself with a few ground rules in advance. First, learn which species of animals are most likely to be seen near the park roads during the season of your visit. Learn what time of day they are most active, how to recognize them, and where to look. Natural history field guides will help. This book gives a few guidelines for spotting some prominent species. Also by learning the park's major natural communities or wildlife habitats it is possible to find the wildlife associated with them. In Yellowstone these wildlife habitats include the following:

Grassland-sagebrush Community: Uinta ground squirrel, pronghorn, jackrabbit, badger, coyote, grizzly, bison; mule deer, whitetail deer and elk in winter.

Willow-cottonwood-sedge Valley Bottom: elk, bison, moose, muskrat, mink, mountain lion, coyote.

Riparian—Lake shore, river and creeks: deer, moose, elk, beaver, muskrat, rabbit, porcupine, river otter, mink, bald eagle, osprey, pelican, garter snake.

Coniferous Forest: snowshoe hare, lynx, red squirrel, black bear, pine marten, porcupine, moose.

Upland Herb-sedge-grass Meadow: marmot, bighorn; mule deer, elk, and bison in summer.

Boreal Meadow: pika, marmot; bighorn in summer.

Sharpen your powers of observation. Listen as well as look. Be alert for the raven's croak, the trumpeting of swans and sandhill cranes, the honking of geese, and the eerie cry of the loon. Mammals, too, can sometimes be detected by voice—or scent, for that matter. Listen for the coyote chorus—which sounds like a pack of yelping puppies. The bugling of the bull elk resounds throughout the park in fall, and the squealing of cow and calf elk in summer may alert you to their presence in the vicinity.

Be an early riser, and an early diner. This will enable you to be out in the first light of day and in the last light of evening, when wildlife watching is at its best for many species. Always, as you drive, have others in your car scan

---

Those magical mornings. Getting up before dawn is not pleasant, but for spotting and photographing wildlife, the quality of low-morning light adds deep, rich color to the landscape. Wildlife, including elk (left), also are out in the open and more visible for viewing and photography. Second only to those magical mornings are evenings.

Bighorn sheep ewes (overleaf) clamber on the slopes of Mount Washburn after resting in isolated niches during the day.

the edges—where the meadow and forest meet.

And remember, parks aren't zoos; satisfaction comes not from quantity, but from the thrill of spotting—by accident or by using your "woods" skills—an animal behaving in its natural surroundings as a free creature of the wilderness.

Spring and fall seasons offer the greatest rewards in watching or photographing Yellowstone's wildlife. These seasons offer several practical advantages. Most of the hoofed browsers and grazers disperse and move into the less-accessible high country in summer. In spring, fall, and winter they can be found in greater concentrations and in more accessible localities. Autumn foliage and winter snows lend color and contrast to your animal pictures. A snowy background also makes most animals stand out more clearly, an advantage in spotting and photographing them. Not the least of the reasons for coming to Yellowstone in the off season is that fewer visitors are in the park to disturb the animals or get in the way of your lens.

Photo Tips

Except for photographing larger animals spotted near the roads, telephoto lenses will be an advantage. A 35-mm camera with a 100- to 500-mm lens is perhaps the most practical choice for photographing small birds and mammals or for portraits of large animals. For habitat shots, a normal or wide-angle lens is fine.

Elk—also called wapiti by Shawnee Indians, in reference to their light-colored rump patch—stand up to five feet tall at the shoulders and weigh as much as 1,000 pounds.

With extremely bright light prevailing on sunny days in Yellowstone, you will not generally need fast films. In fact, you will be wise to guard against overexposure. But in the early morning and the evening hours when wildlife watching is at its best, you'll have good use for fast-emulsion films, but a sacrifice for grain quality.

When photographing a backlighted animal or one that is in the shade of trees, allow for greater exposure. A meter reading or automatic exposure influenced by a bright sky or foreground can result in underexposure of a moose or mule deer browsing in the forest edge.

Be thoroughly familiar with your camera and have it ready to capture those great shots that come unexpectedly, as when you pull your car to the side of the road because a moose is crossing and you want to get a photograph before it disappears into the forest.

Your car can serve at times as an observation station or photography blind. Many wild animals that take flight at the approach of man on foot will tolerate his presence at close range in an automobile. Coyotes, for example, will sometimes come close enough for a camera portrait. For safety's sake, too—as when photographing a bear—your car will be the best spot for you. It may pay to drive to the observation site before daylight, choosing your vantage point and parking your vehicle with the expected angle of the sun in mind. You will then have time to set up your camera and be waiting quietly when light reveals the scene. Banging car doors, talking loudly, starting up the motor, and other noisy activity will work to your disadvantage.

A tripod will vastly increase your photographic opportunities, particularly in poor light conditions and when using a telephoto lens. It will help prevent blurred pictures that result from handholding any camera at slow shutter speeds. Shutter speeds necessary to stop movement of an animal depend on such factors as distance and whether the animal is moving toward the camera or across the field of view.

If you lack a long-focus lens you may have

Bighorn rams stand a mere three feet at the shoulders and weigh about 200 pounds. During summer in Yellowstone, bighorn sheep migrate to higher mountain ranges, such as Mount Washburn, then move to lower elevations around the Gardner River Canyon in winter.

to be satisfied with pictures of animals as part of their habitat. It is not safe to approach a bison or other large animal closely enough to get a portrait of it with a normal lens. And never try to put a person in the picture with your wildlife subject. Remember, too, that trying to approach an animal on foot is likely to frighten it and move it back out of view.

THE HOOFED ANIMALS

There are seven species of hoofed mammals, or ungulates, in Yellowstone—bighorn, bison, pronghorn, moose, elk, mule

Bison, misnamed "buffalo" by European settlers, wait out a Yellowstone snowstorm. They are members of the Bovidae family, and both sexes bear permanent horns that are comprised of a bony core covered with a thick horn which is derived from dense skin and hair.

deer, and whitetail deer. Ungulates are the most conspicuous animals in the park, and provide many of the visitor's greatest wilderness thrills. They are accustomed enough to man's presence that you can often watch them at your leisure and at fairly close range. But don't mistake their tolerance of your presence

for tameness. Don't approach them on foot—or try to drive off the road to get closer.

To identify these species, you need know only one or two distinguishing characteristics of each. A pair of binoculars is sometimes essential. Keep in mind that it is difficult to judge distance when you are in unfamiliar surroundings, and identifying by size is unreliable without a known object for comparison.

Bighorn

In Yellowstone, the bighorn, or bighorn sheep, may be a leftover from an earlier postglacial time, when favorable habitat was much more extensive, supporting a larger population than presently exists. The bighorn is well suited to steep, rocky, sparsely wooded slopes and rocky mountain summits. Today, with a more moderate climate, forests have increased, true alpine areas are limited to the highest peaks, and the bighorn population is limited.

In summer the bighorn migrate to the higher reaches of the northeast sector of the park—Mount Washburn and the Absaroka Range. You can see those on Mount Washburn by hiking the road or trail to the top. In winter most of the bighorn migrate to lower elevations, becoming especially concentrated in the area between Mammoth and Gardiner, on the base of Mount Everts. They are often seen above the road in Gardner Canyon, on the cliffs of the Yellowstone River near Tower, and on the slopes above where Soda Butte Creek enters the Lamar River. In Grand Teton they are occasionally seen in the Teton Range, but

Bison possess massive neck muscles that allow them to use their heads like snowplows to move deep snow, accessing hidden forage below. Nonetheless, winter is a stressful time for ungulates.

the best location, especially during the winter and spring, is in the Gros Ventre Range along southern exposed slopes.

Because bighorn occupy a specialized habitat—steep, rocky slopes—to which few other animals are so well adapted and which these bighorn sheep use for escape, they are relatively invulnerable to predators. When migrat-

ing, however, they must cross territory where their surefootedness is of no special advantage, and may be taken by mountain lions or other large predators. Lambs, during their first week or two of life, are subject to predation even by coyotes.

Bighorn are easily distinguished from other Yellowstone ungulates. Both sexes show a conspicuous white rump patch. The rams weigh about 200 pounds, have massive horns curling a partial to a full circle. Ewes are smaller, and their smaller horns curve slightly backward.

Bison

Yellowstone's bison are some of the last wild, free-ranging bison in the United States, where they once numbered 60 million on the Great Plains. These bison are descended, in part, from the only wild bison in the United States to survive the time of near extinction during the late 1800s. Although the mountain bison of Yellowstone survived, they were poached to such low numbers during the early decades of the park's existence that plains bison from captive herds were introduced to Yellowstone in 1902. The hybrid descendants from both subspecies have retained the hardiness and behavior patterns of the original mountain bison.

The bison herds are most easily seen where roads cross wintering areas where they concentrate in the valleys of the Lamar and Firehole rivers and Hayden Valley. The Lamar road is open all winter; watch for the bison from

Junction Butte to Lamar Canyon, from the end of November through May. On the Firehole River bison are most often found somewhere in the Lower Geyser Basin during winter and summer. Oversnow vehicles provide access via the Firehole road in midwinter. And during the summer Hayden Valley provides the best opportunity for observing large herds. One of the best times to see bison is in May, when the frisky, red, newborn calves cavort about their protective mothers. In summer the herds are in less accessible meadows of the park, but lone bulls are often seen, particularly in small meadows.

Bison were never considered indigenous to Grand Teton. During the early years of the national park a small wildlife enclosure was established near Oxbow Bend for visitors to view wildlife. As maintenance and upkeep became too costly they were turned loose, and today's herd are descendants of those animals.

Pronghorn, misnamed "antelope," are neither true antelope nor true goat, but the last remnant of a spiral- and fork-horned mammal that developed in North Ameria during the Ecocene Epoch. They are the fastest North American mammal, running for short bursts of nearly 55 miles an hour and cruising at 25 to 30 miles an hour.

Bison populations are greatly influenced by winter conditions. Bison are hardy and well-adapted to foraging in fairly deep snow, Their large heads and powerful necks act as snow plows to reach dried grasses buried underneath. But winters are long and periodically quite severe. Mortality resulting from the stress imposed by the combination of deep snows, inaccessible or reduced forage, age, disease, wind, occasional times of crusting, and prolonged storms is important in the natural regulation of the population size. However, winterkilled bison then become a vital food source for grizzly bears, coyotes, ravens, and other scavengers.

Pronghorn
Popularly but mistakenly called an antelope, the pronghorn is actually the only species of its family—a group distinct from true antelopes. This swift and beautiful creature of the plains is one of Yellowstone's animals that

can be seen any time of the year—if you look in the right locations. Its range is limited to the lower, northern region of Yellowstone, in the Yellowstone River drainage. A few pronghorn live the year around on the flats in the Gardiner, Montana, area and on slopes on either side of the Gardner River toward Mammoth Hot Springs. In Grand Teton during the summer they are often found on the sagebrush-flats of Antelope Flats and migrate into the Gros Ventre Range during the winter.

In spring many pronghorn migrate up the Yellowstone River, across Blacktail Plateau and eventually into the Lamar River valley and the junction of Soda Butte Creek with the Lamar River. But for a short grazing animal there is too much snow in these areas in winter; and, among Yellowstone's ungulates the pronghorn is the least tolerant of snow. Before the heavy fall snowstorms, the pronghorn migrates to its main winter range at the north edge of the park below Mammoth.

Since they live on sage and other low-growing shrubs in open dry areas that don't get much snow, and since they depend on fleetness of foot and excellent eyesight for protection from predators, pronghorn avoid the forest. Consequently, they may be seen at any time of day.

Although both males and females bear horns and have conspicuous white rump patches like the bighorn, they are easily distinguished. Pronghorn are smaller, adults weigh about 100 pounds. Their erect, slightly branching, black horns curve backward only at the tip; the tan and white body markings are more striking; and they occupy relatively level, open grassland habitats rather than steep, rocky slopes.

The pronghorn, like the bighorn, may once have been more widely distributed in Yellowstone. A warmer period some centuries ago may have created habitat conditions favorable to pronghorn even in the central part of the park. Today pronghorn numbers as well as distribution have shrunk. Changes in habitat, decreasing availability of winter range, and some of man's activities have all affected the pronghorn population.

Moose

This large, awkward, photogenic animal is often found along riparian water courses. It is a permanent resident, but Grand Teton is the southern extent of its range (recently, however, moose have been introduced into Colorado). Its long legs enable it to manage quite well in 'moose muck' and deep winter snows. Moose are not herding animals; you will see loners, family groups, and occasionally several bulls together. Look for them in broken forest and in willow-covered meadows. In Yellowstone they are often seen in summer in Hayden Valley and near the mouth of Pelican Creek; and in winter, between Tower Junction and the Northeast Entrance. In Grand Teton they are often found during summer and winter in the Willow Flats area near Jackson Lake Lodge.

The moose is the largest member of the deer family and the males, or bulls, possess large

antlers. Its great size and formidable hooves make the moose relatively secure against predators other than wolves and grizzlies. Its humpbacked body on stilt-like legs, big head with pendulous muzzle, and massive, palmate (broad-bladed) antlers make the moose recognizable at a great distance. The cow moose, antlerless and less massive, is easy to distinguish from other members of the deer family by her long legs, heavy shoulders, and big muzzle.

The moose maintains itself in winter by browsing or eating the bark and twig ends of willows, birch, and aspen and other shrubs and occasionally the needles of subalpine fir, Douglas-fir, and other conifers. It is principally a browser on land, but is often seen in summer

Long-legged and graceful, moose (left), the largest member of the deer family, are right at home among Yellowstone's and Jackson Hole's willow thickets and river bottoms whereas elk (above) have adapted to open meadows and forests. Both are members of the deer family and grace antlers, which are derived from bone. Antlers are grown and shed each year only by males.

standing in water several feet deep, plunging its head under the surface to feed upon bottom-rooted aquatic plants.

Studies indicate that the wolves of Isle Royale National Park subsist almost entirely on the moose herd. But it is not known to what extent wolves prey upon Yellowstone's moose. Grizzlies may take a few. Moose can be quite belligerent, and bulls during the fall rutting season, or cows with calves, tend to be ill-tempered. Play it safe, and keep your distance.

American Elk (Wapiti)

Mention Yellowstone wildlife to anyone and he may first think of "elk." And with good reason, for this is the most abundant large game animal in the parks. The elk is almost moose-sized, but it is majestic rather than ungainly in appearance. The bull's great, spreading antlers are not palmate like the moose's, and both males and females have a large, buff or pale-yellow rump patch that distinguishes them from other hoofed animals.

The elk is both a browser and grazer, feeding upon a wide range of vegetation including sedges, grasses, and other herbs, various shrubs, willows, the bark of aspens, and the needles of Douglas-fir and subalpine fir. This species, probably totaling more pounds of flesh than all the other ungulates in the park combined, is important in the ecosystem as a consumer of plant life and as food for predators and scavengers. It is

preyed upon by mountain lions and by grizzlies, and coyotes may take some fawns.

Traditionally elk migrate to lower elevations during the winter and the elk population in the parks is less; in summer Yellowstone and Grand Teton is home to many more. In the Greater Yellowstone Ecosystem are four main herds. The large southern herd descends into Jackson Hole and winters over at the National Elk Refuge where they are given supplemental feed. This large herd, numbering from 7,000 to 12,000 animals, is easily viewed just outside the town of Jackson. Most of the Gallatin herd leaves in winter, too, going down the Gallatin River Valley. The Madison herd generally does not leave the park, but remains in the Madison River drainage throughout the year.

'The mule deer earns its name from huge ears that are two-thirds the length of its head. These sensitive ears aid in detecting danger. When alarmed, their black-tipped tail (hence their other common name—black-tail deer) raises as a signal to others, and they stot—a stiff-legged bounce with all four feet off the ground—to safety.

In Yellowstone it is the northern herd that provides the great wildlife show for winter visitors. Part of this herd moves outside the park in winter, but many remain on the south-facing slopes of the Yellowstone River drainage and on exposed slopes that don't become snow covered. Look for them in late fall or winter on the road from Gardiner to Cooke City. In summer elk frequent the area between Mammoth and Norris. The best times of the day to see large numbers of elk from a road is early morning before they have been "spooked" by traffic, or late evening. They are not easy to spot when they're among the trees, but look near the forest edge. Binoculars will help in scanning distant open slopes.

Mule Deer

A large summer population of mule deer is scattered throughout Yellowstone, except in dense forests. Look in broken forest and small meadows for this small member of the deer family. Browsers rather than grazers, mule deer feed principally on shrubs and coniferous trees. There is plenty of food for them in summer, but mule deer can't tolerate deep snow, so most migrate out of Yellowstone in winter. The small winter population is augmented in spring by individuals returning from Jackson Hole to the south, the Shoshone River drainage to the east, the lower Madison River valley to the west, and the Yellowstone River valley in the north. In

winter you can see large numbers in and near the park, around Mammoth Hot Springs down to Gardiner and beyond.

In Jackson Hole they are common summer and winter residents. During the summer they can be found in the higher meadows and canyons of the Teton Range, but they migrate to lower meadows and south-facing buttes for the winter.

Mule deer are preyed upon by mountain lions and grizzlies, and probably by the park's few wolves. Fawns and disabled adults are also vulnerable to coyotes.

You should have no trouble recognizing this species. The mule-like ears, black-tipped tail, body form and size, and bouncing, bounding gait set it apart from the other ungulates. Males have antlers which branch equally, and are not pronged from a main beam. Their summer coat is a reddish tan and their winter coat is grayish, dark brown, tipped with black.

Whitetail Deer

This is the smallest of Grand Teton and Yellowstone's four members of the deer family; it weighs less than one-quarter as much as the moose, one-third as much as the elk. It is very similar to the mule deer, but the whitetail deer prefers forests and dark woods. It is also primarily a browser, living on shrubs during the winter and grass and herbs during the summer.

A large white flag, or tail, wagging back and forth and disappearing into the woods indicates a whitetail deer is on the run. Males, or bucks, sport antlers, which consist of a main beam with prongs. Its white tail and unbranching antlers are the distinguishing features between mule and whitetail deer. However, like mule deer its coat is reddish most of the year, becoming grayish in winter.

Yellowstone and Grand Teton each have a small population of whitetail deer. In Yellowstone during the summer they inhabit the northern section of the park, especially in the Tower-Roosevelt area in dense, old growth Douglas-fir and lodgepole pine forests, and migrate to lower elevations for the winter. However, they are elusive and not very common. Only a small number of whitetail deer inhabit Jackson Hole and these stay mainly in the southern section of the valley. Again, they are difficult to find.

The elusive white-tailed deer, found at the extreme southern and northern ranges of the Yellowstone-Grand Teton ecosystem, has tubular hairs that provide extra insulation and enable the deer to lie on snow without melting it.
The coyote (overleaf), which ranges widely and will eat almost anything, often can be seen stalking small animals in the grassland-sagebrush community.

CARNIVORES

You will see fewer four-footed predators and scavengers in the parks than hoofed animals—not only because they are more secutive, but also because plant-eaters always vastly outnumber the carnivores that feed upon them. Some of the predators of the parks have made a comeback from the days of persecution, some are barely holding their own, and some have maintained good populations. We still have much to learn about the exact role predators play here, but it is clear that their presence is vital to the health of the Greater Yellowstone Ecosystem.

The name coyote (above) comes from the Aztec coyotl, *and its scientific name,* Canis latrans, *means "barking dog." The coyote is famous in lore and legend and rightfully so, as it is a tough, adaptive animal with keen senses and survival instincts.*
The gray wolf (right) once roamed most of the North American continent, though government predator-control programs eliminated the species, except in Canada. But indigenous wolves have been sighted in Yellowstone and, in 1995, wolves were reintroduced.

Coyote

The coyote, which has always been common in Yellowstone, has been abused by people throughout its vast natural range—which even today extends from Alaska to Mexico and from California to Massachusetts. Along with other large predators, it was persecuted during the early years of the park. In a 12-year span at the turn of the century, for example, 2,236 coyotes were poisoned, trapped, or shot in Yellowstone. Since 1934, however, a more enlightened attitude toward predators has prevailed, and the coyote has rebounded to its former abundance.

This wild canine functions in the park ecosystem as a predator on ground squirrels, pocket gophers, meadow voles, and other small mammals and as a scavenger on larger

animals that have died or been killed. While the primary factor controlling populations of herbivores is the supply of plant foods, the coyote's role may tend to even out the fluctuations in numbers of rodents and hares, minimizing the chance of overpopulation that could unbalance the ecosystem.

Coyotes are among the least finicky of animals. They eat primarily voles, but, also grass,

unmolested, have become accustomed to the presence of people. You may see them by the roadside, and one may even approach your car out of curiosity. Look for them in the drier, larger open areas—sagebrush and grassland—and especially in Yellowstone in Hayden Valley, Lamar Valley, Tower, Mammoth, and the Blacktail Plateau, while in Grand Teton the National Elk Refuge is the best location. And be sure to listen for them at night.

Don't confuse this medium-sized wild dog with the much larger wolf. Your chances of seeing the latter are remote. The wolf is far warier than the coyote, and is extremely rare in the park.

Wolf

The wolf, perhaps the most maligned, most persecuted mammal in America, is now gaining a measure of compassion and respect. Moderate numbers of wolves were present in the

The red fox is an opportunistic and omnivorous mammal. It is very common along the outer edge of the ecosystem, but deep snow and severe winters limit it from establishing in the higher, mountainous interior of the Rocky Mountains.

insects, fruit, carrion, fish, birds, mice, hares, porcupines, and frogs.

The coyotes of Yellowstone, where they are

early years of Yellowstone. But in those days—when even some biologists subscribed to the belief that "the only good predator is a dead one"—it was trapped, poisoned, and shot mercilessly. By 1926 it was thought to have been eliminated from Yellowstone National Park. Controversy still rages whether indigenous wolves still exist in Yellowstone, but records indicate, however, that there have always been a few wolves present in Yellowstone or its immediate vicinity. Costly campaigns and lobbying lead by the National Park Service reintroduced wolves again into Yellowstone in 1995. A similar reintroduction of the plains bison at the turn-of-the-century altered Yellowstone's indigenous population of the woods bison. But, it is not known what effect the introduction of an alien wolf gene poses on the Greater Yellowstone Ecosystem.

The wolf in Yellowstone, as elsewhere, no doubt has a culling effect on the ungulates it hunts, by weeding out sick, weak, or crippled individuals—those easiest to overtake and subdue. But Yellowstone's small wolf population today has little impact on the populations of hoofed animals.

Don't expect to see a wolf in the park; but if you're there in the spring keep a weather eye out for it. However, wolves are very similar in appearance to coyotes and their identification even fools experienced biologists. There is nothing to fear if you do encounter one, for no wild, nonrabid North American wolf has been known to attack a person.

Red Fox

The red fox is the wiliest and the newest member of Yellowstone and Grand Teton's wildlife. They are not abundant, but in recent years have increased their range and are often found in the northern section of Yellowstone and in the Grand Canyon area. In Grand Teton they are common in the southern end of the valley and occasionally on the National Elk Refuge. They are especially very abundant outside of the parks surrounding the Greater Yellowstone Ecosystem.

The Red Fox is generally reddish yellow with black legs, but its coat is often spotted with black streaks. During the winter its coat and tail is thick and healthy, but in the spring and early summer its coat is patchy and shedding. By summer its coat is thin and the red fox appears as a lanky, lean member of the dog family.

Red foxes are primarily active at night in open country and sparse forests, but early morning and late evening is the best time to observe them. They feed on insects, birds, rodents, rabbits, and fruit.

Pine Marten

The pine marten, as its name suggests, inhabits the coniferous forest. The most arboreal of weasels, it preys upon squirrels and birds, as well as ground-dwelling rodents, shrews, and pikas. It is one of several members of the weasel family in Yellowstone (others include: skunk, fisher, both shorttail and longtail weasels, mink, otter, badger, and wolverine).

You may encounter a marten when hiking

Weasels

An inquisitive, playful predator found in wooded areas, usually not far from water, throughout the Greater Yellowstone Ecosystem.

The short or longtail weasels have adapted to camouflage, like the snowshoe hare. Their summer coat is dark brown with a yellowish underside. But in winter their pelage turns white, except for its black-tipped tail, and takes on its winter name of ermine.

There is nothing more thrilling than to watch a playful weasel romp around down timber or among rock. Enjoy their comical antics while you can before they suddenly disappear as quickly as they originally appeared.

River Otter

A delight to watch, this large, playful, so-

Pine martens (above) are at home in mature coniferous forests. Their monkeylike antics—jumping arboreally among the tree tops—and their bright orange throat patch distinguish them from their close cousin, the weasel (right). The weasel sports a sleek brown coat during the summer but wears white in winter. The winter pelage gives weasels their other name—ermine.

or camping. Don't mistake its seemingly friendly behavior for tameness—it is probably mere curiosity that makes this 2-pound carnivore appear so sociable. A hardy animal, it neither hibernates nor migrates to lower levels in winter. It is seldom far from the forest. Identify it by its mink-like form, prominent ears, bushy tail, and buffy-orange chest spot.

cial member of the weasel family is not a common species in Yellowstone, but keep a sharp eye for it around West Thumb during the winter and the outlet of Yellowstone Lake and the inlet of Pelican Creek during the summer. Like bald eagles, ospreys, and pelicans, the otter is dependent on fish, especially cutthroat trout.

Imagine the excitement of watching a curious otter poke its head out of the water alongside your canoe in Yellowstone Lake or seeing a frolicking otter family in one of

Sleek and agile, a river otter is adept at chasing and catching fish in water. During winter, along the banks of the Snake River, otters toboggan on their bellies. When there is no snow, a slippery, muddy bank will do.

Yellowstone or Grand Teton's ponds! Look for these slender animals in the Oxbow of the Snake River in Grand Teton, as well as along the edges of lakes and ponds.

Mountain Lion

This sleek, graceful, sinewy cat is generally called cougar in the Rockies. In other sections of the country it goes by the name puma, painter, panther, or catamount. An estimated 100 mountain lions lived in Yellowstone in the first decade of this century, but they were almost wiped out during the prolonged anti-predator campaign in this region. For reasons we don't fully understand, they have never recovered, and are so scarce now as to have little impact on the park's ecology.

These big cats are always associated with deer—in fact, they are unknown outside of deer range—and in Yellowstone probably subsist chiefly on mule deer, though they will take smaller mammals. Years ago, however, in Yellowstone mountain lions apparently depended upon elk as a major food source. To the extent that elk numbers and distribution on the northern range can again duplicate conditions that prevailed during early decades of the park's existence, the mountain lion may in time increase. Occasionally mountain lions are spotted in Grand Teton and most of the sightings originate along the Gros Ventre Mountains.

Only by the sheerest accident will you see a wild mountain lion. They are very rare,

elusive and secretive and very few people have seen one—except hunters using dogs to tree their quarry. If by remote chance you do encounter a big cat with a long tail, this is it. But don't be alarmed; a wild mountain lion is never a threat to man.

Black Bear

Although classed as a carnivore, the black bear is actually, like humans, an omnivore. It eats fruit, flesh, fish, and fowl, as well as grass, insects, roots, and carrion. Most of its diet during the year is more vegetarian than meat-eating. Black bears prefer forested habitats, but they are constantly moving in their never ending search for food.

Today, people who visited Yellowstone years ago when roadside bears were commonplace ask, "Where are the bears?" The change came about in the early 1970s because park service managers imposed a ban on feeding and, with the elimination of park service open pits used for garbage disposal forced bears to return to natural ways—digging, picking, grazing, foraging, and hunting for their food. It is true, this abrupt ban has had serious repercussions

---

The rare and elusive mountain lion seldom is seen in the northern Rocky Mountains, but it does inhabit northern Yellowstone and the Gros Ventre Mountains of Jackson Hole. Mountain lions have specialized canines that seize and perforate prey and carnassials, or special cheek teeth, that cut like scissors.
Grizzly bears (overleaf), also seldom seen in the ecosystem, frolic in the waning autumn sunshine before winter storms drive them to hibernation.

on the stability of the black bear population, and fewer bears are seen today along the roadside; but when you do come upon one, you will be seeing an animal foraging rather than roadside begging.

You can tell the black bear from the grizzly by its generally smaller size; more pointed head with straight, not dished, profile, and lack of shoulder hump. Black bears are not always black; a single litter may contain one black, one brown, and one cinnamon-colored cub.

Grizzly

Perhaps one-fourth of the grizzlies remaining in the contiguous United States are in the Greater Yellowstone Ecosystem. There is concern that this big bear, to many the symbol of the American wilderness, may be vanishing from the earth. While you are not likely to see one in Yellowstone during the peak of the visitor season, it should give you a measure of satisfaction just to know that you are in grizzly country—to know that here at least they are given protection. The small population of grizzlies—its population is not exactly known, but probably numbering less than 200—is restricted primarily to Yellowstone National Park. It is not, like the black bear, primarily a forest animal, but its home range is larger and it requires more space. There are certain open areas close to traveled routes where it may be seen digging for roots or rodents.

The grizzly is not ordinarily a hunter,

tracking and pursuing a selected victim, but is in fact more vegetarian than carnivore. In spring, it comes out of its long sleepy period 2 or 3 weeks earlier than the black bear. At this time elk and mule deer are likely to be weakened from the rigors of winter, with some individuals on their last

is to watch a grizzly in spring as it grazes on new green grass, turns up sod to get at roots, bulbs, and rodents, or tears apart rotting logs for ants. Spring spawning of the cutthroat and other trout give these bears the opportunity to indulge in a favorite food. Watch for fishing grizzlies in the Pelican Creek area, the Yellowstone River outlet of Yellowstone Lake and Grant Village.

Later in the season, when the surviving elk and deer are in good shape again and moving to higher country, the grizzly depends largely on bulbs, sedge, green shoots, whitebark pine nuts, moths and berries.

Black bears once were a common sight and a Yellowstone symbol, but today are a rare sight. Black bears are not always black, but come in a wide range of colors from black to cinnamon, tan and brown. They are recognized easily by their lack of shoulder humps and their long, straight snouts.

Your best opportunity to see grizzlies is from the road in spring when they are feeding in the valley bottoms. They are widely distributed in the back country, and

legs. Easy kills, as well as carcasses of dead ungulates now emerging from the melting snows, provide an abundance of meat and carrion from early May until mid-June.

One of Yellowstone's greatest wildlife thrills

precautions should be taken when hiking and traveling through grizzly country.

Grizzlies, as long as they remain truly wild, tend to flee from people's presence. They usually smell or hear approaching humans, and leave without being seen. The most dangerous encounter is an accidental surprise that startles the bear. To avert such occurrences, make noise whenever on foot in grizzly territory.

When camping in bear country, camp near trees if possible; adult grizzlies have difficulty climbing trees. Keep food out of your tent and out of reach of bears, and keep a clean camp. Sows with cubs are also overly protective, give them extra space and avoidance. Never fail to give these powerful and unpredictable animals a great deal of respect. Remember, in Yellowstone you are the visitor—in one of the few homes left to the grizzly bear.

GNAWING ANIMALS

Gnawing animals, including both the rodents and the hare-and-rabbit order, are the most abundant of Yellowstone and Grand Teton's mammals, with more species and larger populations than any other groups.

Grizzly bears once were the denizen and emblem of wilderness, but now are scarce in the Yellowstone-Grand Teton ecosystem. During the 1988 Yellowstone fires, very few grizzlies were sighted, and the Yellowstone grizzly may be headed toward extinction. The name "grizzly" refers to its grizzled coat, which typically is dark brown with a grizzly frosting on its back (which are long, blonde-colored guard hairs), the source of their nickname, "silvertip." The grizzly is recognized by its prominent shoulder hump and its short, saucer-shaped profile snout.

Consequently, they are close to the core of the park's web of life. They are almost entirely herbivorous, though some rodents devour

quantities of insects and other invertebrate life, and a few species prey upon small birds or even upon smaller rodents. Most importantly, they provide a staple diet for predators ranging in size from shrews—the smallest of mammals—to grizzlies, the largest of the flesh eaters.

Pika

This tiny, almost tailless cousin of the rabbits and hares is a hardy individualist. Its home is often the park's severest environment, the rockslides close to timberline, and this accounts for another of its names—rock rabbit. In Yellowstone listen for its telltale buzzy *pee...* near the summit of Mount Washburn, or in the Golden Gate area. Open rockslides of Cascade Canyon, or any of the canyons, of Grand Teton provide excellent habitat for pikas; then look for it scurrying for the safety of a rock crevice.

In summer the pika busily gathers twigs, leaves, grasses, sedges, and other green plant

Rock rabbits or pikas (top) and snowshoe hares (bottom) may be in different families but they are closely related. Both are lagomorphs, meaning "hareshape." Hares, however, are characteristically longer-legged and possess a keen sense of hearing, enchanced by large, independently swiveling ears. Pikas are rock-dwellers and harvest grasses and other plants that sustain them through winter. Snowshoe hares have adapted to winter with large snowshoe-like hind feet that support their weight on snow. They also have the ability to change their color with the seasons—brown in summer and white in winter.

matter, which it piles beneath a jumble of rocks. In winter it lives snugly but actively among the rocks beneath the snow, subsisting on these haystacks. During its daytime summer foraging for plants it is vulnerable to weasels and pine martens. Hawks and ravens sometimes pounce on a pika that has strayed too far from the safety of its rock pile.

Snowshoe Hare

The snowshoe hare is also called the varying hare. During the summer its pelage, or coat, is dark brown with black-tipped ears. Its coat changes to snowy white with black-tipped ears in winter. And in the spring and fall it often appears mottled brown and white. This adaptation provides camouflaging and protection from predators. Another adaptation for deep snow country are its large, wide, snowshoe-like hind feet that give it support.

Even though the snowshoe hare does not hibernate, its adaptations allow it to survive harsh winters. It feeds primarily on buds, twigs, bark and frozen carrion. While they in turn, also provide subsistence for predators, including coyotes, fox and birds of prey. Snowshoe hare are also known for their boom and bust population cycles which in turn directly effect the well-being of its predator populations.

Uinta Ground Squirrel

Like other ground squirrels, this rodent is often called "picket pin," from its habit of sit-

This family group of Uinta ground squirrels will spend most of their lives underground and asleep. They emerge from their burrows in late April or early May, but only remain active—eating and avoiding predators—until mid-August, when they disappear into their burrows, sealing up the entrances and not emerging until the next spring. Another similar species overlaps the range of the Uinta ground squirrel, but the Richardson's ground squirrel's tail is buff and the Uinta's is gray.

ting upright, looking much like a peg driven into the ground. Another name is "chiseler," for its trill-like call. Your attention may first

be attracted by its voice—a descending, bird-like squeal. This burrowing animal lives almost entirely on stems, leaves, flowers, and seeds of green plants. It is preyed upon by hawks, ravens, weasels, badgers, foxes, and coyotes. The chiseler is associated in Yellowstone with sagebrush, but not in wet soils. Look for it in Yellowstone at Lamar, Tower, and Mammoth, and in Grand Teton around buildings and developed sites. But since it goes into hibernation as early as mid-August and doesn't come out until late-May, its active season is about the shortest for any Yellowstone vertebrate.

Three small mammals are common inhabitants of the Yellowstone-Grand Teton ecosystem. The arboreal red squirrel (top) eats almost anything, but its favorite foods are fungi and mushrooms—which are dried on pine boughs and stored in crotches of limbs—and lodgepole pine nuts—which are harvested and stored in the ground, usually under rocks and holes, to ripen. The golden-mantled ground squirrel (middle), may look like a large chipmunk, but its lifestyle is very different. The golden-mantled ground squirrel collects and caches food in its burrow and, by October, curls up in its den and hibernates. The yellow pine chipmunk (bottom) is half the size of the golden-mantled ground squirrel. It prefers above-ground nests during the summer, but by early winter finds more suitable accommodations underground, where they venture in and out during winter, depending on temperatures.
The yellow-bellied marmot (right) lives in colonies, and usually is at home under a rock slide with a large boulder nearby for sunning and observing. Their sharp, piercing whistle alerts the colony that an intruder is near.

Red Squirrel

A lodgepole pine forest cannot be entered in Yellowstone or Grand Teton without the distinctive and vocal chatter of a red squirrel. The red squirrel is very territorial and when another squirrel or a human enters its domain it sends out a threatening call.

The red squirrel is active all year and has a distinct winter and summer rusty red coat, with a white underside. Although its summer coat is a darker reddish gray with black side stripes and its winter coat is a pale rusty gray. It feeds on lodgepole pine nuts and mushrooms which are also stored for winter use.

Yellow-bellied Marmot

This rodent, similar to but larger than its eastern cousin, the woodchuck or groundhog, is adapted to open rocky slopes where grass is plentiful. It is common in high country, but Yellowstone visitors more

often see a marmot along the road through Golden Gate, at Storm Point on Yellowstone Lake, or along the road between Mammoth and Tower, and among the rock slopes in the canyons of Grand Teton.

The marmot is one of the winter sleepers, retiring as early as September and coming out of hibernation in June, when it may have to burrow through snow to reach daylight. During that part of the year in which it is active a marmot is likely to be seen at any time of day sunning itself on the most prominent boulder in its grassy domain. A sharp, shrill alarm whistle may be your first hint of its presence.

Porcupines do not throw their quills. When a predator ventures too close, the porcupine positions its back and raises its quills against the threat; with a quick movement of its tail, hundreds of quills may embed themselves in the snout or paw of its aggressor. But some predators, such as the fisher, have become adept at avoiding quills.

Porcupine

No other animal in Grand Teton and Yellowstone appears as clumsy as the porcupine. They are seen lumbering through the forests, or hunched into what appears to be a big black ball in a tree. Even though they appear awkward their long, sharp

44\

quills lend all the protection they need from predators.

Muskrat

One of the most widely distributed of North American mammals, known in every State but Hawaii, the muskrat occupies many of the ponds, lakes, and larger rivers of the parks. Look for the muskrat's lodge—a conical mound of aquatic-plant stalks, more symmetrical and much smaller than the house of sticks and mud built by the beaver. Although it shares its aquatic habitat with otter, beaver, and mink, the chances are that a small mammal with a ratlike tail you see swimming in the Yellowstone or Snake rivers or almost any pond or marsh will be a muskrat.

Along with its principal diet of leaves, stems, and roots of aquatic plants, the muskrat eats frogs, salamanders, and an occasional fish. In turn it is preyed upon by otters, coyotes, and bald and golden eagles.

Beaver

This industrious four-footed, flat-tailed, engineer—builder of dams, lodges, and canals—is the creator of habitat favorable to an array of mammals, birds, fish, and amphibians. There is visible evidence that beavers were abundant in Yellowstone in former years: the remnants of dams (including one that was thought to be the world's largest beaver dam—which you can see in Yellowstone from the

Beavers are primarily nocturnal, working diligently at night to construct and repair dams, canals and lodges. In autumn, they collect branches and saplings that are jabbed into the bottom of the pond. As winter seals over its pond with a layer of ice, beavers retrieve their stash by submerging, sometimes up to 15 minutes, under the ice.

road near Obsidian Cliff, between Norris and Mammoth) and the many meadows that appear to have been formed through natural succession from abandoned beaver ponds. Today these big, busy rodents are found in the park in relatively small numbers. Biologists are not certain of the reason for their apparent decline. You can still see active lodges and dams, and if you're lucky you may see one of the builders.

Beavers are vegetarians, feeding upon aquatic plants in addition to the twigs and tender bark of trees they cut. They are preyed upon by a number of carnivores—in Yellowstone and Grand Teton, by coyote, wolf, mountain lion, lynx, and bobcat. But beavers are more important as environmental engineers than as links in the food chain.

Voles

Mouse-like voles in Yellowstone and Grand Teton outnumber any other mammal, and provide the primary sustenance for the park's carnivores. Most, like the meadow vole are active

Voles (above) are prolific breeders and fall prey to a legion of predators, from owls to bears and coyotes and even fish. Voles outnumber all other animals and perhaps make up the largest biomass in the ecosystem.

The northern flying squirrel (right) lives in old-growth coniferous forests, but seldom is seen. They come out of their cavity nests at dusk, lunging into space and spreading membranes between their limbs, and glide, maneuvering with legs and tail and braking before landing on a perch. Their nighttime foraging is a search for pine nuts, larvae, seeds, berries, insects, fungi and an occasional baby bird.

either day or night. Their presence can be detected by narrow runways, approximately an inch or two wide, through matted grass and sedges. Runways lead to grazing areas where short pieces of grass blades can be found. Other evidence is visible by detecting small piles of brownish droppings.

The short-tailed meadow vole prefers low moist areas near streams and lakes. They are considered good swimmers and during the winter they burrow through snow and emerge from small round entrances. Once exposed on the snowy surface they are easy prey for large birds.

A close relative to the meadow vole is the boreal redbacked vole. Their preferred habitat comprises old growth forest where the gray, short tail, reddish back vole can often be found cruising its runways.

BIRDS

Endless hours of bird-watching pleasure and excitement are yours if you come armed with a good field guide and a pair of binoculars. With well over 200 species known in the parks, we can suggest here only some guidelines for a few of the prominent species. The parks' water birds—fish-eating birds of prey, wading birds, grebes, gulls, shore birds, ducks, geese, and swans— offer particularly rewarding watching. Look on and over the ponds (especially at Lamar and Christian Pond), lakes, rivers, and marshes. Hayden Valley is the best area in Yellowstone and, Jackson Lake and Oxbow Bend is the best in Grand Teton.

The four-foot-tall great blue heron (left) stalks its prey through the shallows or stands poised like a statue, waiting for an unsuspecting meal to venture near. Great blue herons nest in colonies, and their cluster of platform nests can be spotted in the tops of trees near the water's edge. White pelicans (above) also form colonies, called pods, and nest on remote, barren islands in Yellowstone Lake. Pelican chicks are born blind and naked from their shell, and they huddle together for warmth and protection from the elements while their parents are out foraging. Adults do not capture and hold live fish in their lower bill's pouch for their young. Instead, a pelican chick rubs its bill along the base of its parent's bill to stimulate regurgitation directly into its own craw.

White Pelican

This huge white bird, with a 9-foot black tipped wingspread, is another of America's threatened animals. The decline in numbers of pelicans appears to have been primarily agricultural pesticides that were acquired by way of the fish they ate during their southward migration and wintering period. In Yellowstone and Grand Teton pelicans are summer residents only. Their breeding colonies on the Molly Islands in the southeast arm of Yellowstone Lake are secure—for that part of the lake is off limits to motorboats, and not even canoes are permitted to approach within one-quarter of a mile of the islands.

Identify flying pelicans—often at great heights—by black wing tips, head hunched back on shoulders, and its long, flat bill resting on its curved neck. During breeding season its bill develops a protruding knob on top. Look for them drifting along the Yellowstone River and on Yellowstone Lake, and on the Snake River at Oxbow Bend and Jackson Lake in Grand Teton.

The white pelican relishes trout, which it scoops up in its basket-like bill while foraging in the water. Pelicans are social birds and raise their young collectively in groups called pods.

Trumpeter Swan

One of America's rarest birds, the beautiful trumpeter can yet be seen by almost any alert visitor. It breeds here in summer; and some swans remain in the parks through the year, in areas where there is open water.

There has been an unknown cyclic cause why very few nesting pairs have successfully raised young in Yellowstone. Its habitat is protected in Yellowstone, Grand Teton and nearby Red Rocks Waterfowl Refuge and this is a key factor in survival of this species, so long feared on the way to extinction.

Trumpeter swans (top) are the largest of all swans and once were found in large numbers throughout the West. They were nearly brought to extinction by overhunting, but nesting swans (bottom) now have made a comeback and are a common sight in this region.

The great wingspread of the bald eagle (right), which spans seven feet, and its powerful, deeply curved talons are evident. Bald eagles are primarily scavengers, but they also are excellent fishermen.

Look on the larger lakes of Yellowstone, on the Madison and Yellowstone Rivers, and in Hayden Valley. In Jackson Hole, Flat Creek, Oxbow Bend and Christian Pond are prime locations. The trumpeter can be distinguished from the whistling swan—a migrant and winter resident but not a breeder in the parks—by its much louder, lower-pitched, more bugle-like voice. Especially if you have a long-focus lens, this photogenic bird will be a prime subject for your camera.

Bald Eagle

A generation ago the bald eagle, our national symbol, was widely distributed over America. Today the pleasure of watching this great bird as it soars high on almost unmoving wings is rare, outside of Alaska. It can often be found along lake shores and rivers and often scavenges fish from osprey or white pelicans.

Not even in Yellowstone and Grand Teton, once ideal sanctuaries for this wilderness bird of prey, is the bald eagle abundant today. The chief reasons are habitat loss, guns, poison, and environmental pollution—primarily pesticides, which is accumulated in the eagle's tissues from the fish it eats. Unfortunately, Yellowstone's eagles face these dangers as soon as they leave in the fall on their migratory routes—often migrating toward the Oregon or Northern California coast. However, some individuals remain in the parks through the year.

Since its principal food here is trout and carrion look for the eagle at Lake, Hayden Valley, the lower valley of the Yellowstone River, the Madison River, the National Elk Refuge, and along the Snake River. In spring this eagle, which is a scavenger as well as predator, can be seen feeding on thawing carcasses of deer or elk that have perished during the winter. And in the spring they build, or return to, large bulky nests atop towering pines or cottonwood trees.

As spring brings colorful flowers, it also brings colorful birds. Mountain bluebirds (top) often can be seen during summer in the grassland-sagebrush community, hovering over their prey—chiefly insects—before dropping to catch them. Another colorful summertime visitor is the western tanager (middle)—rare, but an inhabitant of coniferous forests. The Stellers jay (bottom) also is a forest inhabitant, seen dropping from branch to branch and calling out a harsh series of shaacks.

Osprey

Like the bald eagle, the osprey is a fisherman—a more skilled one, in fact. And like the bald eagle its numbers declined during the middle of the 20th century from the effects of guns and pesticide pollution. The osprey is still fairly common in Yellowstone and Grand Teton from late spring, when it arrives from the south, until the fall freeze. It is frequently seen at Yellowstone Lake, in Hayden Valley, and in Yellowstone Canyon. From any of the canyon overlooks, watch for the ospreys soaring back and forth over the river; you may spy one going to its nest perched on a rocky pinnacle on the side of the canyon. They can also be spotted in the Oxbox Bend area of Grand Teton and around many of the lakes and rivers.

Well adapted for its way of life, this distant relative of the falcon lives exclusively on fish captured by plunging feet first into the water. Although its head is largely white, it should not be confused with the adult bald eagle, whose head and tail are both entirely snow-white with the rest of the body dark. The osprey is dark brownish above and clear white below, the only large bird of prey so marked.

Magpie

Eastern visitors to the parks often ask about this strikingly patterned bird seen in the West. It is not as-big-bodied as a crow, but its very long tail gives it the impression of great size. Watch for it in Yellowstone especially in the lower Gardner and Yellowstone River valleys, and along Slough Creek and the Lamar River

No other bird is identifiable to the West as is the black-billed magpie. Its unusual black and white markings and long tail with iridescent green highlights are distinguishing characteristics. A loud whining maag *and a series of harsh* queeks *also are typical.*

and in ranching areas of Grand Teton. It's the only large black-and-white land bird with a long tail.

Like the larger raven, the magpie is a scavenger, feeding on any animal carcasses it can find, and is an occasional predator on small animal life. It is a very intelligent bird and is known as a trickster of the bird world.

Raven

The big, jet black bird you see throughout Yellowstone and Grand Teton is the raven. Not to be confused with its smaller cousin the crow, which is much less common here. A raven flies with hawklike alternate flapping and soaring. It has a shaggy neck and a wedge-shaped tail, and it croaks rather than caws. In spring a flock of ravens can alert you to a dead elk or other carcass, for they are scavengers and often feed alongside coyotes or even grizzly bears. During the spawning season you may see them feeding on fish washed up on the bank.

Dark brown above, white on the head and belly, and a prominent dark eye stripe differentiate the osprey (right) from the bald eagle. The osprey eats fish almost exclusively and can be found somewhere near water. The raven (far right), however, is found in almost every habitat. Even though it resembles an American crow, it can be distinguished by its larger size and its wedge-shaped tail during flight.

COLD-BLOODED VERTEBRATES

Unless you are a fisherman, you are likely to be unaware of Yellowstone's cold-blooded vertebrate animals. The most abundant—and ecologically important—cold-blooded vertebrates are the fishes. Less than a dozen species of reptiles and amphibians live here, and these are not, in most areas of the parks, numerous enough to play a significant role in the ecology.

Not surprisingly in a region lying above 6,000 feet at this latitude, the environment supports only five species of snakes—and of these only one species of garter snake is widely distributed. Also present are bull snakes, rubber boas, and, in a very limited area near Gardiner, the prairie rattlesnake. One lizard, the sagebrush liz-ard, is most commonly seen near thermal areas, especially Norris and Shoshone geyser basins.

Amphibians are represented by more species, and some are present in fairly large numbers in places. The western toad occurs in a variety of habitats. Listen in early summer for the tiny chorus frog, which is abundant in some wetlands below 8,000 feet. This and

Ideal habitat for Yellowstone-Grand Teton ecosystem's cold-blooded vertebrates, especially cutthroat trout, is clear, cold, rocky-bottomed streams and clear, deep lakes (left). In spring, cutthroat trout (above) move into inlet streams to spawn. Males migrate first and vie for arriving females. Females then fight among themselves for ideal spawning sites—a well-aerated gravel bottom, and a temperature averaging 52°F. She then digs a nest four to 10 inches deep into the gravel bottom with powerful thrusts of her tail. Both male and female align over the nest (or redd) to deposit and fertilize the eggs. After all of the nearly 1,000 eggs have been laid, the female fills the depression with gravel from upstream.

other frogs can be identified by their voices, like the songs of birds. The voiceless tiger salamander is common, and may be seen on wet evenings in summer, when it is found at or near its breeding ponds. Look for it particularly at the ponds in the Lamar Valley in Yellowstone and Willow Flats in Grand Teton.

As cold-blooded animals, amphibians and reptiles must hibernate, and can be seen only in the warmer months, if at all. Some are so scarce—or, like the rubber boa, are so secretive in their habits—that you may have difficulty finding them.

Always keep in mind that, in these national parks, all species of vertebrates, from eagle to coyote to snowshoe hare to garter snake to toad, are protected. The only exceptions are fish caught according to National Park Service regulations. It is your right to enjoy Yellowstone's wildlife, and your responsibility to respect their sanctuary.

The Yellowstone-Grand Teton ecosystem has several subspecies of cutthroat trout (top), named for red marks on their lower jaw. After long foodless winters, grizzly bears rely on cutthroat trout in spring, as the fish spawn up the smaller streams. White pelicans subsist on cutthroat trout during their summer sojourn, and river otter depend on the trout for their winter nourishment. Mountain whitefish (below), considered by some a delicacy, also are natives.

Yellowstone's thermal springs (right) may seem like ideal habitat for cold-blooded vertebrates, but most springs and geysers average nearly 190°F (boiling point for this elevation is 199°F). Only bacteria live in the hottest springs. As the water cools in the runoff channels, however, wildlife are able to use the warmth provided by the thermals. The sagebrush lizard is the only lizard species associated with the thermal basins and found at this high elevation. During winter, bison and elk move in to use the snow-free environment and, occassionally, the warm steam.

PROTECTING WILDLIFE HABITAT

Wildlife biologists recognize today that there is nothing so important in wildlife preservation as maintaining good habitat. This means an environment in which all the basic needs—food, water, air, breeding grounds, shelter from the elements, protection from enemies, and living space—are available in sufficient quantity and quality. An inadequate supply of just one of these will affect the health and stability of an animal population. Living space, in the case of large browsers and grazers that move from the high country to the lowlands in fall, can be a problem even in a large ecosystem as Yellowstone—for the historic winter range of some animals may lie outside the park boundaries, in lands that are fenced for domestic stock or open to hunting.

"Living space" entails also the freedom from crowding or disturbance by humans. Human development has the largest impact on wildlife and in effect deprives them of needed nesting, feeding, and resting areas.

Winter and early spring in Yellowstone cannot be surpassed for offering countless opportunities to see and photograph wildlife. Snow forces elk, deer, bison, and bighorn down from their high country summer range to the valley bottoms and surrounding open slopes, many of which are adjacent to park roads. Only at this time of year can you get a true impression of the huge numbers of Yellowstone's animal populations, which in summer are distributed over a much larger area of the park.

But at any time of year Yellowstone presents one of North America's classic wildlife displays. Very few places remain where a visitor can thrill to the sight of the magnificent trumpeter swan, watch wild bison grazing in an open meadow, or just know that he is a guest in one of the last domains of the trumpeter swan and the grizzly bear.

Habitat is one of the most important requirements to sustain healthy wildlife populations. Within the northern Rockies, a wide range of habitats are required, especially riparian (above), mountain habitats with open meadows and nearby forests, such as Mount Washburn (left), and migration routes and valleys as found on the National Elk Refuge in Jackson Hole (overleaf).

Other Yellowstone and Grand Teton books by HOMESTEAD PUBLISHING

YELLOWSTONE: SELECTED PHOTOGRAPHS 1870-1960
with introduction by Senator Alan Simpson, edited by Carl Schreier
GREATER YELLOWSTONE'S FUTURE *by Tim Clark and Steven Minta*
MATTIE: A WOMAN'S JOURNEY WEST *by Nan Weber*
HIKING YELLOWSTONE TRAILS *by Carl Schreier*
YELLOWSTONE EXPLORERS GUIDE *by Carl Schreier*
GRAND TETON EXPLORERS GUIDE *by Carl Schreier*
HIKING GRAND TETON TRAILS *by Carl Schreier*
A FIELD GUIDE TO YELLOWSTONE'S GEYSERS, HOT SPRINGS AND FUMAROLES
by Carl Schreier
TETON SKIING: A HISTORY AND GUIDE TO THE TETON RANGE, WYOMING
by Thomas Turiano
THE GRAND TETONS: THE STORY OF TAMING THE WESTERN WILDERNESS
by Margaret Sanborn
BONNEY'S GUIDE TO JACKSON'S HOLE AND GRAND TETON NATIONAL PARK
by Lorraine Bonney